THE ETHICAL SPEAKER

AN ETHICS HANDBOOK FOR NATIONAL SPEAKERS ASSOCIATION CERTIFIED SPEAKING PROFESSIONAL (CSP) APPLICANTS

Margarita Gurri, PhD, CSP

with Dave Bricker, MFA

THE ETHICAL SPEAKER

AN ETHICS HANDBOOK FOR NATIONAL SPEAKERS ASSOCIATION CERTIFIED SPEAKING PROFESSIONAL (CSP) APPLICANTS

by Margarita Gurri, PhD, CSP

with Dave Bricker, MFA

All Rights Reserved.
Copyright 2016

This book may not be reproduced, transmitted, or stored in whole or in part by any means, including graphic, electronic, or mechanical without the express written consent of the publisher except in the case of brief quotations embodied in critical articles and reviews.

ISBN: 978-0-9862960-0-0
Printed in the United States of America
Cover and book design by David Bricker

Red Shoe Media
1-954-609-9904 (Eastern Time)
Margarita@RedShoeInstitute.com
RedShoeInstitute.com

DEDICATION

"Just do the right thing."
— Joseph N. Gurri, MD

This little book on ethics is for my father
whose ethics were simple, but not easy.

CONTENTS

"Successful people are willing to do things that unsuccessful people are unwilling to do. Practice. Ask questions, Go the extra mile. Keep your word."
— *Joachim de Posada, PhD, Global CSP*

Contents i
Introduction 1
Ethical Foundations 3
Ethics and the Law 9
Why Do We Misbehave? 13
The NSA Code of Ethics 19
Representation 25
Professionalism 29
Research 35
Intellectual Property 39
Respect & Collegiality 47
Confidentiality 51
Business Practices 55
Diversity 59
The Ethical Side of the Street 63

Speaker Resources 65
Appendix A - Ethical Foundations Worksheet 71
Appendix C - Three Levels of Thinking 79
Appendix D - Ethical Decision-making Worksheet... 83
Appendix F - Author, Margarita Gurri, PhD, CSP 89
Appendix G - Author, Dave Bricker, MFA 93

"The ultimate measure of a man is not where he stands in moments of comfort and convenience, but where he stands at times of challenge and controversy."

— *Dr. Martin Luther King, Jr.*[1]

---

1. King, Martin Luther, Jr. *The Measure of a Man*. Education Press. Pathfinder Books, 2015.

INTRODUCTION

If you aim at nothing, you will hit it every time."
— Zig Ziglar[2]

This little book for ethical speakers was created as a handbook for participants in the NSA Influence 2016 Ethics Competency Course as a high level introduction to the eight principles of the National Speakers Association's Code of Professional Ethics.

BE THE ETHICAL SPEAKER YOUR DOG THINKS YOU ARE!

Even the best professional speakers struggle with ethical dilemmas. Your professional reputation is about who you are, what you do, and how you do it. It takes seconds to create a first impression, months to sculpt a reputation, and an instant to destroy it. What do colleagues, clients, and vendors say about you to your face and behind your back?

The National Speakers Association's ethical principles offer guidance as we strive to master the Four Es:

2. https://www.ziglar.com/articles/if-you-aim-at-nothing-2

2 THE ETHICAL SPEAKER

Expertise, Eloquence, Enterprise, and Ethics. For practical speakers and for those not so ethically driven, it is wise to note that ethics are *profitable,* improving our brands and enhancing our individual and industry reputations.

OBJECTIVES

In the spirit of Cavett Robert, CSP, CPAE, this course fulfills one of three requirements for the Certified Speaking Professional (CSP) designation.

Participants will:

- Explore ethical principles for professional speakers
- Understand why people misbehave
- Practice ethical decision-making
- Create an Ethics Awareness Plan

PROFESSIONAL CONFLICT OF INTEREST DISCLOSURE

Professional business practice requires a declaration of conflict of interest or no conflict of interest. Other than my love of chocolate, I have nothing to disclose.

ETHICAL FOUNDATIONS

"You wear your choice on your face. Take a look."
— *Beba G. Gurri*

My father's view of ethics was simple, not easy. "Just do the right thing." He believed that acting honorably was part of our obligation to help create a better world. As naturalized citizens, my parents, Joseph N. Gurri, MD and Beba G. Gurri instilled in the four Gurri children the importance of giving back in gratitude for the freedom afforded us by the USA, our adopted country.

Everyone receives unique ethical foundations from family, faith and educational communities, and global experiences. These values inform our choices in good times and bad.

WHAT ARE ETHICS?

Ethics are society's effort to understand the effect of morality and moral standards on our conduct. Ethics provide a way to know what the "right thing" to do is when it counts the most.

Ethics exist because good behavior does not always pay. Ironically, in the real world, virtue is not always the easiest course toward tangible reward. As seen so often in the news, illegal and unethical behavior often pays well.

Vows, pledges, oaths, promises, policies, agreements, and procedures are formal ethical guidelines. Informal guidelines or social mores usually go unwritten and are often unspoken. When we cross a cultural more, we know it from the disapproval expressed by others. Talk during a movie; other viewers nearby quickly advise you verbally and nonverbally that you have violated a commonsense ethical code of conduct.

ETHICAL SPEAKERS

In the spirit of Cavett Robert, CSP, CPAE, ethical Speakers invite, support, and stimulate colleagues to work within agreed-upon guidelines for conduct that serve the greater good. While virtue is no guarantee of success, for speakers, it is a necessary foundation for it.

A strong ethical foundation is especially important for professional speakers who impact cultures globally and locally, in business, and in the community. What we say and how we say it matters. Speakers motivate, innovate, and offer perspective to individuals and organizations, creating ethical strategies for achieving excellence. Speakers lead leaders. Ethical leadership strengthens our own bottom line, that of our clients, and that of the economy.

Ethical Professional Speakers rely on bylaws and professional codes of ethics to establish and maintain a reputation for professionalism and integrity. Knowledge of and adherence to professional codes are conditions of National Speakers Association membership. These codes of ethics set standards to further the reputation of each speaker, the association, and the speaking industry.

Committing to ethical behavior as members of a premier organization for professional speakers makes us stronger personally and professionally, and fosters pleasant, meaningful, successful lives and relationships.

WHY ETHICS?

"Virtue is its own reward." Research and common sense have shown that organizations committed to the highest standards of conduct and ethics produce superior results.

6 THE ETHICAL SPEAKER

One of my favorite speakers is our NSA President, Ruby Newell-Legner, CSP[3]. A 7-Star Service expert, Ruby knows that reaching for and achieving high standards creates superior service and stellar reputations.

WHAT IS ETHICAL?

Six simple and practical guidelines are posed by George May[4] to discern the ethical choice. Before you act, ask yourself about:

Values

Does your action follow the spirit of the law or principle?

Conscience

Can you justify your action to yourself or someone you respect?

---

3. Newell-Legner, Ruby. www.7starservice.com.
4. May, George. Business Ethics Guidelines and Resources.

Rules

How does your planned action fit with policies and procedures?

Laws

Is the action legal?

Heroes

How would your hero act?
Would he or she blame others?

Promises

Will your action live up to your promises?
Will it build trust?

8 THE ETHICAL SPEAKER

ETHICS AND THE LAW

"This is a book that nobody wants to read, but everyone should."
— *Caroline de Posada-Rodriguez, Esquire*

The history of ethics and the law is all about boundaries; fairness; protecting individuals and groups from harm; and preventing conflicts of interest, fraud, and theft. Consider the overlap between ethics and the legal code. Ethics are based on a higher level of expectation for conduct; the law is the *lowest* level of conduct expected by society or a group.

What is acceptable to do or not to do, say, or not say? Speakers are bound by local, national, and international laws; active contracts; and laws that apply to their chosen professions. The following are some key laws and legal principles that help guide speakers to choose ethical actions, interactions, and communications on their path toward excellence:

Americans with Disabilities Act (ADA) Compliance
Breach of Contract or Duty
Client Information and Confidentiality
Code of Ethics and Statutes for Public Officers
 and Employees
Copyright Infringement
Defamation
Discrimination Complaint Procedures and Laws
Diversity Management
Employment Practices
Environmental Issues
Equal Employment Opportunity Commission (EEOC)
Ethical Business & Management Practices
Fraud Laws
Harassment Laws
Harm to a Person's Dignity
Hostile Workplace Laws
International Business Laws
Negligence and Misconduct
Quid Pro Quo Laws

Political Involvement

Professional Licensure

Sexual Conduct and Harassment

Social Media and Media Practices

Vendor Relationships

Violence and Other Intentional Wrongs Against
    Other People

12 THE ETHICAL SPEAKER

WHY DO WE MISBEHAVE?

"Make failure your teacher, not your undertaker."
"It's not how far you fall, but how high you bounce that counts."

— *Zig Ziglar*[5]

Few people set out to intentionally disgrace themselves, incur fines or jail sentences, get fired, or be censured by their colleagues and industry.

So, why *do* we misbehave?

A complicated array of internal and external factors contributes to our decisions to act ethically or not. As a consulting psychologist for over thirty years, I've found that people misbehave for altruistic reasons, and in response to "delicious temptations."

Consider four altruistic reasons and four seductive motivators for unethical behavior. Then, consider internal and external factors that make us vulnerable to unethical choices and behavior.

5. Zig Ziglar. https://www.ziglar.com

ALTRUISM

Good people sometimes lose jobs, go to jail, pay fines, face financial ruin, and destroy their reputations by "helping" someone in need. One way to combat this generous impulse is to ask yourself, "Will this course of action wrong anyone? Is it something I can shout proudly about to the world? Is this going to make the recipient of my goodwill a better, stronger person, or does it just bail them out of their own poor planning and weak choices?"

If these questions fail to inform your decision to "help" someone in questionable ways; ask yourself, "Would I even consider asking anyone to do this *for me?*" Overly kind, generous people who can't resist helping others are not likely to even consider asking others for the same favors.

Four altruistic, unethical favors are common to good people:

1. Cutting corners
2. Turning a blind eye
3. Hiding the truth for or from others
4. Giving overly generous or false feedback

"DELICIOUS TEMPTATIONS" THE BIG FOUR[6]

Enticed by lucrative fees and fame, and shaken by pressure to succeed, speakers are sometimes motivated to overlook ethical values. "Delicious temptations" contribute to slippery thinking and unethical behavior. Ethicist George S. May said it best: We act unethically due to:

1. Greed
2. Speed
3. Laziness
4. Haziness

Whether motivated by altruism or temptation, truth and trust are destroyed when we behave unethically.

> "Because we have an image (simulacrum) of ourselves as fair, objective, practical, and humane, we actually make it more difficult for ourselves to be what we think we are."
> — Thomas Merton[7]

---

6. May, George. Business Ethics Guidelines and Resources.
7. Merton, Thomas. Faith and Violence. Notre Dame, Ind: University of Notre Dame Press, 1968.

WHAT MAKES US VULNERABLE TO UNETHICAL BEHAVIOR?

Ethical choices and behavior are complicated. Consider some factors that influence our choices.

INTERNAL FACTORS

Feelings

Anger, hunger, desperation, anxiety, frustration, fatigue

Entitlement

"Why not me? I deserve this more than the other person?"

"I'm special. Why should the rules apply to me?"

"Why shouldn't we hold this person accountable? Are they special?"

Culture

Internalized family values, neighborhood, workplace cultures, faith communities

Mind Games

We can convince ourselves of many things that aren't true

Bitterness

"They owe me"

"Why am I getting blamed for this? It's not fair!"

"It's time for payback!"

EXTERNAL FACTORS

Pressure

Social, emotional, financial, being helpful, being needed

Opportunity

Isolation, privacy, independence, poor security controls

Culture

Culture of acceptance in family, neighborhood, workplace, associations

Finances

Desperation, shame, financial distress can misdirect our values and commitments

THE NSA CODE OF ETHICS

"In looking for people to hire, you look for three qualities: integrity, intelligence, and energy. And if they don't have the first, the other two will kill you."
— Warren Buffet,[8] CEO, Berkshire Hathaway

Speakers exert a great deal of influence over the lives of individuals, organizations, and communities locally and globally. With such impact, it is critical that we *get it right*.

NSA Founder, Cavett Robert, CSP, CPAE created a culture of excellence for global speakers. "The Spirit of Cavett" is a call to action for speakers to help one another in the quest for high standards. The NSA Code of Ethics guides us along the path to mastery of the four Es of Speaker Competence: Eloquence, Expertise, Enterprise, and Ethics so that we can make a lasting, positive impact.

Motivational Speaker, humorist, and leadership expert Tim Durkin, CSP, reminds us that the "NSA Code of Professional Ethics is a *continuing* condition of membership;

8. Buffet, Warren *Thoughts of Chairman Buffett: Thirty Years of Unconventional Wisdom from the Sage of Omaha.* Harper Business; 1st edition, 2011

it is *not* just one of the four competencies that can be taken in degrees." The NSA Codes of Ethics are reproduced below for easy reference.[9]

NSA CODE OF ETHICS[10]

The purpose of this Code of Professional Ethics is to establish and maintain our brand, reputation, and public confidence in the professionalism, dedication, and integrity of individual members of NSA, and the Association itself.

The characteristics of honesty, leadership, and stewardship are integral to the success of NSA and the individual professional speaker.

Therefore, all members of NSA subscribe to this Code of Professional Ethics as a condition of membership, with the firm belief that each member will strive to uphold the values, reputation, and legacy of NSA. By doing so, members recognize the necessity to preserve and encourage fair and equitable practices among all who are engaged in professional speaking.

9. Durkin, Tim, CSP http://TimDurkin.com.
10. National Speakers Association. From the NSASpeaker.org website, June 2016, http://nsa.org

Violations of this Code are determined in accordance with the bylaws, policies, and procedures of NSA. Any disciplinary action instituted by NSA shall be binding and final upon the NSA member and without recourse to the Association, its officers, members of staff."

ARTICLE 1 – REPRESENTATION

The NSA member has an obligation to oneself and to NSA to represent oneself truthfully, professionally and in a non-misleading manner. The NSA member shall be honest and accurate in presenting qualifications and experience in the member's communication with others.

ARTICLE 2 – PROFESSIONALISM

The NSA member shall act, operate his/her business, and speak in a most professional and ethical manner so as neither to offend nor bring discredit to oneself, the speaking professional, or one's fellow NSA members.

ARTICLE 3 – RESEARCH

The NSA member shall exert efforts to understand each client's organization, approaches, goals, and culture in advance of a presentation in order to professionally apply one's expertise to meet each client's needs.

ARTICLE 4 – INTELLECTUAL PROPERTY

The NSA member shall avoid using — either orally or in writing — materials, titles, or thematic creations originated by others unless approved in writing by the originator.

ARTICLE 5 – RESPECT AND COLLEGIALITY

The NSA member shall maintain a collegial relationship with fellow members that is based on respect, professional courtesy, dignity, and the highest ethical standards.

ARTICLE 6 – CONFIDENTIALITY

The NSA member shall maintain and respect the confidentiality of business or personal affairs of clients, agents, and other speakers.

ARTICLE 7 – BUSINESS PRACTICES

The NSA member is obligated to maintain a high level of ethical standards and practices in order to assist in protecting the public against fraud or any unfair practice in the speaking profession, and shall attempt to eliminate from the profession all practices that could bring discredit to the speaking profession.

ARTICLE 8 – DIVERSITY

The NSA member shall not participate in any agreement or activity that would limit or deny access to the marketplace to any other speaker, to a client, or to the public. This includes, but is not limited to, economic factors, race, ethnicity, creed, color, sex, age, sexual orientation, disability, religion, or country of national origin of any party.

24 THE ETHICAL SPEAKER

REPRESENTATION
ARTICLE 1 NSA CODE OF ETHICS

"Be impeccable with your word."
　　　　　　　— *don Miguel Ruiz, The Four Agreements*[11]

The ethical speaker is honest and transparent, and does not mislead or allow misrepresentations to stand uncorrected. Honest representation is all about being genuinely comfortable in our own skins, with our choices, accomplishments, limits, and missteps. It's about being honest and accurate in presenting our qualifications, experience, and expertise in all methods of communication.

THE CASE OF THE MARLBORO MAN

A Phillip Morris and Company Marlboro ad campaign created by Leo Burnett Worldwide offers a tragic example of misrepresentation. With scientific research noting harmful effects of smoking, filtered cigarettes were pitched as a "safer alternative" to unfiltered cigarettes.

---

11. Ruiz, don Miguel. *The Four Agreements.* Amber-Allen Publishing; Box edition, 2008

Unfortunately, filtered cigarettes were not safe. With pseudo-science, complicated terminology, and the emergence of the Marlboro Man, ads helped calm fears of smoking by encouraging the public to buy into filters as a means of risk-reduction. Rugged cowboys, at one with nature, swept past public perceptions of filters as feminine. According to *The Los Angeles Times*,[12] several Marlboro Men died young of smoking-related diseases.

RIGHTING A WRONG

One of the Marlboro Men, David Mclean, who died of lung cancer, became an anti-smoking activist, testifying on behalf of anti-smoking legislation. Another, Eric Lawson, who died of Chronic Obstructive Pulmonary Disease (COPD) appeared in anti-smoking commercials and publicly discussed the harmful effects of smoking. Wayne McLaren, who died of lung cancer, participated in anti-smoking campaigns until his death at the age of 51.

---

12. Pierce, Matt. "At Least Four Marlboro Men Have Died of Smoking-Related Diseases." Los Angeles Times. http://latimes.com/nationnow/la-na-nn-malboro-men-20140127-story.html.

His last words are reported to have been, "Take care of the children. Tobacco will kill you, and I am living proof of it."

THE CASE OF THE SOUND SLEEPER

This gem is from motivational leadership and business speaker Mary Kelly, PhD, CSP, Commander USN (ret.),[13] who says, "Doing the right thing makes it easier to sleep at night."

"In 2009, I heard a speaker use a point in one of his talks that I had used since 1983 in the Navy. He also put it in one of his books. What did I do? Whenever I mention that point, I also say, 'Speaker/author Blah Blah includes this in his book, *XYZ*.' He was the first person who published it, so I give him credit. That is also how it works in academia. You may not be the first person with an idea, but if you are the first to publish it, you get credit. Taking the high road isn't always the easiest road, but it is the right thing to do."

---

13. Kelly, Mary, PhD, CSP, CDR, USN (ret), productiveleaders.com

COMMENTARY

In **The Case of the Marlboro Man,** the actors and real cowboys were asked to misrepresent the facts regarding the safety of a product. Resisting potential rewards that come with misrepresenting our qualifications, our values, life experience, military experience, or the facts are all ethical challenges that come with some lucrative speaking opportunities. In this case, the Marlboro Men demonstrated that it's never too late to do the right thing. We all make mistakes. It's what we do next that counts. What would you do if asked to speak up for something you knew was harmful or not right?

In **The Case of the Sound Sleeper,** Mary demonstrates a key point of the principle of representation. Honest representation goes beyond transparency regarding our credentials, to the source of our research and stories. Knowing her ethical and legal obligations, this speaker was able to take the high road, even when her imitator was not.

PROFESSIONALISM
ARTICLE 2 NSA CODE OF ETHICS

"Wait a minute! 'Unprofessional' is NOT the opposite of 'professional'; it's 'amateur'."

— Jay Izso, Internet Doctor[14]

Professionalism is about taking the high road and going the extra mile.

NSA Founder Cavett Robert, CSP, CPAE knew that the speaking profession would only grow if members worked together in a spirit of community. To encourage professionalism and collegiality, November 14th has been designated as the Spirit of NSA Day. On this day, speaker members are asked to actively encourage peers, refer colleagues to clients, and serve as mentors to emerging speakers.

The heart of professionalism for the ethical speaker is revealed by how we deal with ourselves, clients, vendors,

---

14. Jay Izso, Internet Doctor, *The Opposite of Professional is Not Unprofessional.* https://www.linkedin.com/pulse/opposite-professional-unprofessional-jay-izso-internet-doctor.

and colleagues — how we act, conduct business, and speak to others. The ethical speaker does not offend or discredit him or her self, others, clients, or our industry. Professionalism extends beyond appearances to the quality of our work and relationships.

THE CASE OF THE HOSPITAL GOWN KEYNOTE

This story comes from my mentor, the late Dr. Joachim de Posada, Global CSP as told by his daughter, Caroline de Posada-Rodriguez, Esq. It demonstrates excellence in business and character. As Bruce Turkel[15] said in his beautiful tribute at Joachim's Life Celebration, everyone felt they had "a special relationship" with Joachim. He was the consummate speaker and mentor.

> "My dad battled cancer for many years while he underwent surgeries and treatments. In the last years of his life, he started suffering complications. A few days before a keynote for a Connecticut high school graduation, he went to

15. Turkel, Bruce, Global CSP. *All About Them, Grow Your Business by Focusing on Others.* Da Capo Lifelong Books, 2016.

the ER suffering from severe abdominal pain. He was hospitalized with a bowel obstruction and required a feeding tube up his nose. This meant he would be unable to deliver his keynote presentation to the high school graduates. He was so committed to his purpose in life, that he just couldn't fail those kids. He immediately contacted the high school principal to advise him of what was happening. Despite reassurances from the principal that they would find an alternate speaker, my father was not willing to break his commitment. He grabbed his iPad and instructed me to begin recording. As he sat on his hospital bed in his hospital gown, my father began his commencement keynote. I was surprised because my father had chosen to keep his illness private.

I could not fathom that my father would expose himself to a client in this manner despite the consequences for future engagements that could arise, but my father was a man of his word. He used his own example, showing the new graduates how life will throw them obstacles and curve balls, and how they would have to decide how to honor their commitments. It was the only time my father ever made his illness public. In that instant, he sacrificed his privacy to keep his word. Joachim lived by his principles and in the toughest of times, he walked his talk. As usual, he was a hit!"

THE CASE OF THE RUDE KEYNOTE SPEAKER

I once witnessed a terrific keynoter who, soon after his presentation, could be heard chitchatting loudly at the back of the room — *while another speaker was at the podium.* If that wasn't enough, he was overhead making jokes and uncomplimentary comments about the appearance, slides, and Spanish accent of the speaker who followed him. Though the event planner enjoyed the attention of this well-known keynoter, many of us in the audience were unimpressed. When he was asked to talk more quietly, the speaker blamed the event planner for talking to him, taking no responsibility for his unprofessional behavior.

COMMENTARY

In **The Case of the Hospital Gown Keynote,** Joachim de Posada, Global CSP, demonstrates the importance of having a professional policy for illness, injury, personal emergency, or travel disruptions. Speakers must decide whether they will carry on or hide their illness. Ethics suggests that risking the health of others through exposure to contagious illness is ill-advised.

Calling the client, arranging a back-up speaker, or offering virtual presentations are ethical and professional solutions to the inevitable problems of incapacitation, travel delays, and double-booking. As Joachim would say, "Never compromise one client for another."

What do you include in your client discussion, scope of service documents, and contracts to address the issue of your potential inability to speak as planned?

The Case of the Rude Keynote Speaker goes beyond a manners violation. This is unprofessional behavior. In the movies, nothing is funnier than someone acting unprofessional or petty. We love seeing movie characters use foul language and slurs, dress badly, talk loudly, make annoying sounds, tell offensive jokes, make fun of others, act judgmental, and fail to take responsibility for their actions — but that cluelessness is only funny in the movies.

Bullying, passive-aggressive behavior, and aggressive acts are unprofessional. Words, images, actions, and non-verbal communication that constitutes harassment, sexual harassment, and disrespect of authority or colleagues are additional examples that may also be illegal. A professional speaker must be a professional *listener* who constantly monitors surrounding words and actions, and their own impulsive responses.

How would you handle the rude keynote speaker during the talk and afterward? What would you say and to whom?

RESEARCH
ARTICLE 3 NSA CODE OF ETHICS

"All of your customers are partners in your mission."
— Shep Hyken, CSP, CPAE[16]

Being prepared for a speaking engagement is an ethical requirement and a smart business practice. The ethical professional speaker works hard to understand their client's needs, industry-specific challenges and values, approaches, goals, and culture while preparing for each presentation. Expertise requires ongoing study, research, and observation. Our main point, conclusions, and recommendations must be based on sound experience and fact.

THE CASE OF THE SUPER-PREPARED EXPERT

I once had the pleasure of sharing the stage with Paul J. DiGrigoli at a Beauty Industry Conference. He exploded onto the stage with energizing music and lights, getting the crowd to their feet with simple cues.

---

16. Hyken, Shep, CSP, CPAE. Hyken.com

Before his keynote, he schmoozed with the audience members, asking them about themselves. He listened as they told him about their salons, schools, and products, and he asked questions about what was working and what wasn't for them. A successful owner of Paul J. DiGrigoli Salons, School of Cosmetology and Seminars, and author of *Booked Solid: The Ultimate Guide to Getting and Keeping Clients,* Paul did not rest on his reputation or use his "Standard Keynote." He added value by understanding his audience and their needs, and by clearly and relevantly demonstrating his main point that everyone can turn a negative into a positive.

Afterward, Paul again engaged with attendees, listened attentively, hugged, and posed for pictures with his new fans, and signed his books for hours.

If this were not enough, at my closing keynote, Paul asked if I wanted to "borrow" his music. His interest as a professional speaker was to help the conference be a success by helping *all* the speakers shine. He understood that helping others was in his own best interests. What a professional!

THE CASE OF THE CLUELESS POLITICIAN

A high-profile politician lost her audience and many votes by coming to give a speech unprepared. Repeatedly, she spoke to an audience of public school educators and parents about the challenges and high costs of *private* schooling. What she had to say was well thought-out but offered to the wrong audience. Public school administrators and parents are not concerned about the costs of private education; they face some very different challenges. A little bit of research into her audience's needs and interests would have helped her look like an effective professional speaker and caring public servant. Brand Guru Bruce Turkel[17] says it all with his book title, *"All About Them: Grow Your Business by Focusing on Others."* This speaker forgot that.

COMMENTARY

In **The Case of the Super-Prepared Expert** and **The Case of the Clueless Politician,** the importance of

---

17. Turkel, Bruce. All About Them: *Grow Your Business by Focusing on Others.* Da Capo Lifelong Books, 2016.

understanding your client's needs, challenges, and audiences is noted. Research gives speakers the edge ethically and professionally in providing excellent and meaningful service. No canned speech can meet your client's needs without understanding every audience, every time.

In addition, knowing the venue's quirks and technical specifications is crucial to providing a polished, effective program. How many times have you heard a speaker at the podium saying, "Can you hear me?" as their first words... followed by that ear-piercing squawk that comes from standing too close to the sound system. A little bit of preparation goes a long way.

What do you do before, during, and after you speak to learn your client's culture and needs, and establish your professionalism?

INTELLECTUAL PROPERTY
ARTICLE 4 NSA CODE OF ETHICS

"The best copyright is to be widely quoted."
— *Orvel Ray Wilson, CSP*[18]

Speak your *authentic* truth. This means asking permission to use others' original works and giving credit for any content that is not yours. Getting written permission to use materials, stories, and media in our communications honors the spirit and laws of intellectual property.

This is often not so easy with a cornucopia of "free" material available at a click. Not only does "delicious temptation" abound, it can be difficult to know whether a "free" typeface, image, music track, or video was stolen by the person who made it "free" for you to download and use.

Pirates and poachers are sexy in the movies, but not in the speaking industry. Professional speakers are charged

---

18. Wilson, Orvel Ray, CSP, from CSP Only page on Facebook.

with the task of discerning the origin of these treasures so that they may be properly credited.

Many experienced speakers caution that, "First you hear a story; then you quote it; then you tell it as if it was your own." Familiarity can challenge our sense of ownership. Due diligence is best served when we tell only stories of things we directly experienced or witnessed.

THE CASE OF THE STORY THIEF

Sarah Best, Education Specialist from the NSA team, pointed me to this story: On the CSPs Only Facebook page, the question was asked: Where do you draw the line between *referencing* another person's work or idea, and *stealing* material?

A practical and collegial point of view on story theft comes from Alan Parisse, MBA, CSP, CPAE.[19] "The worst story thieves take other speakers' personal stories and tell them as their own. The best story thieves repeat an idea, share the source of their inspiration, make that

19. Parisse, Alan, MBA, CSP. CPAE. CSP Only page on Facebook.

idea their own, and then expand on it, taking it to a whole new level. That benefits everyone."

I once sat in the audience listening to a speaker as I awaited my turn to give the closing keynote. The speaker spoke of her experience escaping Cuba with her family and of the importance of a positive attitude and grace in the face of adversity. She spoke of her mother wearing red shoes in quiet defiance of Castro. Afterward, I went up to her in the spirit of kinship as this was my own experience and my signature story — The Red Shoe Story. She said, "Oh, it's not my story. I heard it from the Red Shoe Doctor." I was flabbergasted and looked down at my red shoes. She smiled and said, "Oh, it's you! I tell your story all the time." We agreed she could continue to tell the story, but only if she credited it to me.

THE CASE STUDY OF THE "UN-STOLEN" STORY

Caroline de Posada, Esq., daughter of famed global speaker and my mentor, Joachim de Posada, Global CSP, attended a presentation where the keynoter told a story that was identical to a story that appeared in her father's best-selling book. Her first instinct was to confront the keynoter. Thoughts of raising her hand during the Q & A and calling him out naturally occurred to her.

Wisely, she took a few minutes to conduct some online research with her phone, which revealed that this was an old story of unknown origin. Though her father had incorporated this story into his own book, it was not original material, and the speaker had as much right to use it as her father.

COMMENTARY

In **The Case of the Story Thief,** a direct and professional discussion with the story thief resulted in free publicity. This turned out to be a collegial solution to an intellectual property dilemma.

In **The Case of the Un-Stolen Story,** speakers grapple with what is original and what is not. Doing your due diligence is an ethical requirement. What would you do if your signature story or business material was stolen?

Don't assume that everything "freely" available online is actually free. The following tips by Dave Bricker[20] offer guidance with making sound decisions regarding intellectual property rights.

Video

Embedding video can be dangerous as people routinely and illegally post other people's copyrighted material on YouTube. Do your homework on rights owners.

Cartoons and Comics

Cartoons and comics cannot be used in your presentations without permission from their rights holders. Post a picture of Spiderman or Mickey Mouse without permission and you might find yourself in an expensive legal battle with Disney.

Google Images

Most of the images that show up on a Google image search are owned by someone.

20. Bricker, Dave, http:/davebricker.com

Google offers search options for images that are "Labeled for Reuse" and "Labeled for Reuse with Modification." Take advantage of these advanced search features.

Obtaining permission

I once produced a soundtrack for a mattress company video that incorporated a lecture on dreams by an MIT professor. I sampled small bits of the lecture, sent the professor a copy of the track, and received an enthusiastic endorsement in return.

Fair Use

The doctrine of "fair use" in copyright law allows you to sample small bits of media — text, music, images, video, etcetera — for your own purposes. Quoting others' work in this way is legal, but err on the side of caution. Representing other people's work as your own, even by the teaspoon, is risky business. What's "fair" in "fair use" is not clearly defined, and it's best not to have that determination made in a courtroom.

Public Domain

Millions of public domain books, images, films, and other media are available for unrestricted use. Any media with an expired copyright is fair game, making the "vintage look" a safe and charming approach to visual banding.

Royalty-Free Music

If you're a Mac user, consider using Apple's Garage Band® software to create your own royalty-free music tracks. The software is easy to learn and fun to use, even if you know nothing about playing or composing music.

46 THE ETHICAL SPEAKER

RESPECT & COLLEGIALITY
ARTICLE 5 NSA CODE OF ETHICS

"Follow the platinum rule. Treat everyone the way you want them to treat you. There is no place for hate, regret or sorrow. The business and reputation will come back to you."
— *Dr. Gayle N. Carson, CSP*[21]

Be respectful. Be courteous. Any good grandmother would insist on these golden standards to create and maintain collegial relationships with fellow speakers and clients. Professional courtesy builds excellence in our own reputations, our colleagues, and our industry. Customer Service speaker and expert, Shep Hyken, CSP, CPAE[22] gives sound advice, "Be nice. People like to be treated with respect and dignity." This principle goes hand in hand with professionalism by highlighting the importance of relationships.

---

21. Carson, Gayle, PhD, CSP, http://spunkyoldbroad.com.
22. Hyken, Shep, CSP. http://hyken.com

THE CASE OF THE FALSELY ACCUSED COMEDIAN

The following intellectual property story makes a strong case for Respect and Collegiality:

Comedian Amy Schumer was "accused of stealing a fellow comedian's jokes," which resulted in her being vilified on social media. Once the facts were examined, it turned out that the accusations were groundless. The accusing comedian apologized, but the damage was already done. Both comedians' reputations took a hit. Whether or not someone steals from us, ethical speakers handle themselves professionally.

THE CASE OF THE TIME-THIEVING SPEAKER

We have all been at a conference where a time-thieving speaker captivates the audience while eating into the next speaker's time. This demonstrates a lack of respect for the next speaker, the audience, and the client. Stealing time seems innocent enough, but if you're the next speaker you have an ethical dilemma: You were paid for and planned for a 50-minute presentation.

Recently this happened to me. I ended up with fifteen minutes of my planned forty-five. After a quick consultation with the event planner, we agreed I would speak for twenty minutes and offer a forty-five minute webinar the following week as a courtesy. The client was grateful to deal with a gracious professional, and the company is now negotiating to purchase some of my training programs. As my mother always said, "It pays to be nice!"

COMMENTARY

In **The Case of the Falsely Accused Comedian**, the story demonstrates the importance of respect and collegiality even in the face of a potential theft of intellectual property.

Stories are based on common experiences and derived from a limited number of available ideas. Some titles or jokes will inevitably appear to be "borrowed." It is important to give colleagues the benefit of the doubt, and inquire about your concerns in a neutral, collegial way.

Two speakers were once accused of stealing each other's story. It turned out they were both directly involved in that story and had every right to share their own experiences. This happens with like-minded people.

In **The Case of the Time-thieving Speaker,** part of Respect and Collegiality is honoring the client's timeline and sharing the stage professionally with other speakers. Hogging the show is amateurish. Practicing your timing and sticking to the time allotted go hand in hand with being an effective professional speaker.

What would you do if you were the next speaker? Would you continue with your planned program as is? Would you cut your presentation to keep to the schedule? Would you shorten your program and offer to provide a webinar later to deliver the full program? Do you put this in your contract or make verbal agreements with your clients about scheduling and time available before your presentation?

CONFIDENTIALITY
ARTICLE 6 NSA CODE OF ETHICS

"'We have a simple philosophy when it comes to confidentiality — 'nothing; no-one; never.' We don't assume information given to us is confidential; we mandate that it is until otherwise notified. That way we'll never find ourselves in an embarrassing position.'
— Troy Hazard, CSP[23]

Respect the confidentiality of business and personal affairs of clients, agents, and speaker colleagues. Unprofessional sharing and gossip undermine any professional reputation and relationship.

As a speaker, you will witness corporate announcements, speeches, and secrets that outsiders are not normally privy to. Companies must trust their employees to keep these matters confidential, and they must be able to place this same trust in *you*.

You might even be approached by competitors who offer lucrative speaking fees in exchange for disclosure of

---

23. Hazard, Troy, CSP. http://troyhazard.com

what you saw and heard. These companies must be told that though you'd love to speak at their meetings, you'll respect *their* confidential material the same way you respect *all* your clients' — even if that means you don't get the bookings.

THE CASE OF THE NOISY SILENCE

One of easiest ways to violate confidentiality is through social media. A speaker's enthusiastic team posted before, during, and after events. The problem arose when he let his guard down in the face of his eagerness to share his activities and brag about his client's amazing organization. Unintentionally, he breached the company policy of not reporting successes so as to protect their competitive advantage.

Fortunately, when approached with this breach of confidentiality, the speaker took full responsibility and did not blame his team. He consulted with his client and they created an online solution to repair the damage and restore the speaker's credibility with the company, and the company's credibility with the public and their stakeholders.

THE CASE OF THE RUNAWAY TRIBE

Another speaker was especially gifted at building her tribe. The tribe tweeted away during her presentation. During a break, it became clear that the organization's employee audience was breaching confidentiality. Though the speaker is not responsible for the actions of her audience, speakers are thought leaders who can suggest proper and ethical behavior.

When you see audience members posting on public social media during your presentation, you can defend your client's mission by offering a reminder of the confidential nature of the material.

COMMENTARY

In **The Case of the Noisy Silence** and **The Case of the Runaway Tribe,** it is clear that today's ever-growing technology and lightning fast modes of communication facilitate atmospheres where passion can rule out discretion.

Military audiences and innovative companies in competitive businesses require specific understandings about confidentially and safety with regard to speech, email, voicemail, print, video, and social media communication. My father-in-law, the late, Ira A. Glass, Commander USN (ret), a former submarine commander, was fond of the old wartime saying "Loose lips sink ships." On the water or on dry land, this saying offers a mantra for ethical speakers. It is our obligation to learn industry-specific, client-specific, and audience-specific guidelines for protecting confidential information to build and maintain trusting relationships with our clients.

For speakers, marketing can pose a problem. Some clients will not grant permission to use their name or logo in any context, whether in the media, on your website, or in an application. Asking the client is imperative to maintaining trust.

What questions do you ask your clients in order to understand their confidentiality requirements? How do you set an ethical tone for your clients' and audiences' behavior?

BUSINESS PRACTICES
ARTICLE 7 NSA CODE OF ETHICS

"Do what you say you are going to do."
— *Dr. Joachim de Posada, Global CSP*

Be honorable in business. Reach beyond your own conduct to prevent fraud or unfair practice in the speaking profession, and actively work to eliminate all practices that could discredit the speaking profession.

THE CASE OF THE INVISIBLE HONORARIUM

Two unethical practices relate to applicants for the CSP designation. To raise the total fees collected in a year, some speakers accept a booking for an honorarium with the understanding that the speaker will *return* this fee.

Just as unethical is asking a colleague to "hire" you for a presentation given to a few friends, and then misrepresent the context and the fees to help you qualify for the CSP designation. Receiving and returning a check just to pad one's speaking "income" is fraudulent and unethical.

Even talented and experienced speakers are not considered to be *professional* speakers unless they earn speaking fees. The Certified Speaking Professional designation is earned by speakers who have worked hard to master all Four Es: Eloquence, Expertise, Enterprise, and *Ethics*. Let's keep the NSA speaker and CSP brands strong by helping each other shine ethically.

THE CASE OF THE PRICE-FIXERS

Two speakers were contacted by a client. Knowing that whomever was not hired this year would probably be booked next year, the two agreed that neither would lower their speaking fees to compete with the other. By fixing their price, both speakers eventually got their full fee. This is a form of collusion, an unethical practice.

COMMENTARY

In **The Case of the Invisible Honorarium,** anxiety about earning the CSP designation or gaining more business overrides concerns for propriety and sound business practices. Misrepresenting your earnings or trying to pad a resume for the sake of earning a CSP designation is outright fraud against the NSA. It cheapens the CSP and NSA brands and diminishes your own reputation.

What would you say to these misguided speaker applicants? It is best to be kind, tactful, and directly informative. There is no need to sugar coat the unethical or illegal nature of a transgression if one is respectful in the discussion. It is the culture of NSA that speakers help each other achieve excellence. A powerful way to do this is to use mistakes, missteps, and misunderstandings as opportunities to teach and learn.

In **The Case of the Price-Fixers**, price-fixing is illegal and unethical collusion. Price-fixing or the appearance of it is also a legal issue related to anti-trust laws. This is why speakers do not discuss fees in open forums. Questions regarding fees are best addressed to valued mentors and paid speaker consultants. Within a coaching context, fee discussions are healthy and honorable.

58 THE ETHICAL SPEAKER

DIVERSITY
ARTICLE 8 NSA CODE OF ETHICS

Socrates said, "The unexamined life is not worth living." I believe that the unchallenged brain is not worth trusting. While being inclusive might sound easy, in reality, our conscious and unconscious biases can often get in our way.
— *Dr. Helen Turnbull, CSP*

Be inclusive — the more the merrier. Reject any agreement or activity that limits or denies access to the marketplace to anyone. Don't engage in discriminatory practices based on economic factors, race, ethnicity, color, sex, age, sexual orientation, disability, religion, or country of national origin.

THE CASE OF THE SECRET LATINA

When I first started speaking in the 1980s, a faith-based community approached me to create two series of presentations — one on parenting and one on leadership. When it came time to sign the enticing yearlong contract, it was whispered to me that they were looking for trainers for their staff on the topic of diversity. The whisper confused me. Then, I got it; they wanted my help finding a speaker who was not Hispanic.

Thinking they were teasing, I laughed. They stared at me with confusion on their faces. I explained that I thought they knew I was a Cuban-born American and they were being playful with me. They weren't. I bid them a respectful "*adios*" and lost that contract. Years later, they contacted me, asking for help fostering diversity in their quest to create an ethical, inclusive workplace. Standing by our principles helps everyone in the long run.

THE CASE OF THE DROPPED THE MICROPHONE

Dr. Helen Turnbull, CSP, a renowned expert on unconscious bias and diversity, generously offered this anecdote. This is an example of a simple mistake that is a sign of a diversity challenge and opportunity.

> "I remember as if it were yesterday. I was speaking at a conference. My male client and I were working with a male technician to set up the audio equipment. I was introduced

to the technician as Dr. Turnbull and we worked amiably together for about 20 minutes. My client then said to the technician, "By the way, Dr. Turnbull also needs a microphone," to which the technician replied, "I will get *him* one when he arrives." I am not sure whose jaw dropped faster, mine or my client's. Mental models, mind viruses, and unconscious biases are everywhere. The bad news is that they do not go away. The good news is that when you become aware of them, you can make mindful choices and limit their power over you."

COMMENTARY

In **The Case of the Secret Latina** and **The Case of the Dropped Microphone,** ethics and common decency require a discussion of diversity. We all have biases and prejudices. As Dr. Turnbull notes, with awareness, we can "make mindful choices and limit their power" over ourselves and others.

In what ways do you take a stand on the value of diversity? Consider a time when you have benefited from positive biases and been plagued by negative, more limiting prejudices? What is your obligation to educate clients, vendors, and colleagues about diversity?

THE ETHICAL SIDE OF THE STREET
DAVE BRICKER[24]

Ethically, Dave Bricker used the music from a 1930's song, "Sunny Side of the Street", composed by Jimmy McHugh with original lyrics by Dorothy Fields. Some sources credit Fats Waller as the composer who sold his rights for money. Dave used the NSA Code of Ethics to create the lyrics for *"The Ethical Side of the Street."*

VERSE 1

1. REPRESENTATION

Represent yourself as you
Don't exaggerate or embellish
Just direct your honest feet
To the ethical side of the street

CHORUS

When you walk on that stage
With your standards on parade
You'll be all the rage
A speaker: a leader

2. PROFESSIONALISM

Don't insult, offend, or mock
Don't discredit yourself or others
Just direct your honorable feet
To the ethical side of the street

3. RESEARCH

Do your homework on your clients
Meet their needs and expectations
Just direct your customized feet
To the ethical side of the street

---

24. Bricker, Dave, http://www.davebricker.com.

64 THE ETHICAL SPEAKER

VERSE 2

4. INTELLECTUAL PROPERTY

Be clever and creative
Don't plagiarize; give credit
Just direct your original feet
To the ethical side of the street

5. RESPECT

Be friendly and collegial
Be courteous and professional
Just direct your dignified feet
To the ethical side of the street

CHORUS

   When you walk on that stage
   With your standards on parade
   You'll be all the rage
   A speaker: a leader

6. CONFIDENTIALITY

Respect your clients' secrets
Keep it confidential
Quietly direct your feet
To the ethical side of the street

VERSE 3

(guitar solo 8 bars)

7. BUSINESS PRACTICE

Keep your standards high
Keep your business on the level
Just direct your excellent feet
To the ethical side of the street

CHORUS

   When you walk on that stage
   With your standards on parade
   You'll be all the rage
   A speaker: a leader

8. DIVERSITY

Reject discrimination
Be accepting and inclusive
Direct your respectful feet
To the ethical side of the street

SPEAKER RESOURCES

Global Speakers Federation. http://globalspeakersfederation.net, The GSF includes 13 member associations:

1. AFCP, Association Française des EXPERTS & Conférenciers Professionnels. http://www.association-conferenciers.com.
2. APSS, Asia Professional Speakers – Singapore. http://www.asiaspeakers.org.
3. CAP, Canadian Association of Professional Speakers. http://www.canadianspeakers.org.
4. GSA, German Speakers Association. https://germanspeakers.org.
5. IP BRAZIL, Instituto Palestrante - Índice Palestrantes do Brasil. http://institutopalestrante.org.br/indexbase.html.
6. MAPS, Malaysian Association of Professional Speakers. http://www.maps.org.my.
7. NSANZ, National Speakers Association of New Zealand. http://nsanz.org.nz.
8. NSAUS, National Speakers Association. http://www.nsaspeaker.org.

9. PSA, Professional Speakers Australia.
   http://www.nsaspeaker.org/code-of-ethics.
10. PSAB, Professional Speakers Association Belgium.
    http://www.psa-belgium.be.
11. PSAH, Professional Speakers Association Holland.
    http://www.psaholland.org.
12. PSASA, Professional Speakers Association of Southern Africa.
    http://psasouthernafrica.co.za.
13. PSAUKI, Professional Speaking Association UK & Ireland.
    http://www.thepsa.co.uk.

Hazard, Troy, CSP. *Future-Proofing Your Business.* Wiley; 1 edition, 2010

International Association of Professional Motivational Speakers (IAPO). https://www.iapcollege.com/program/membership-motivational-speakers

International Association of Corporate Speakers. http://www.corporatespeaker.org

International Speakers Association. http://speakersassociation.org/InternationalSpeakersAssociations.htm

Professional Keynote Motivational Speaker Ethics.
http://www.difrances.com/ethics.htm

Professional Speakers Association of Southern Africa (PSASA).
http://psasouthernafrica.co.za

Robert, Cavett, CSP, CPAE. *Paid to Speak, Best Practices for Building a Successful Speaking Business*

Greenleaf Book Group Press; unknown edition, 2011

Seidman, Dov and Clinton, Bill. *How: Why How We Do Anything Means Everything.* Wiley; Edition: 1, 2011

Shapiro, Norman and Anderson, Robert H. *Toward an Ethics and Etiquette for Electronic Mail.* Rand Corp, 1985

Toastmasters International Accredited Speakers.
http://www.accreditedspeakers.com/ASCodeofEthics.html

Women Speakers Association (WSA).
http://www.womenspeakersassociation.com

"I thought up an ending for my book.
 'And he lives happily ever after, till the end of his days.'"
  – Bilbo Baggins, JRR Tolkien, Fellowship of the Ring

70 THE ETHICAL SPEAKER

APPENDIX A
ETHICAL FOUNDATIONS WORKSHEET

So often, our ethics go unspoken and unwritten. It's a good day to think and write!

On the following pages, list your top five values or ethical principles. Rate how you are doing at achieving each of them with 5 being "the best I can do," and 1 being, "it's a work in progress."

What are your obligations with regard to each value?

What is the consequence of poorly resolved ethical conflict for each value?

72 THE ETHICAL SPEAKER

VALUE	RANK	OBLIGATION	CONSEQUENCE
1.			
2.			
3.			

ETHICAL FOUNDATIONS WORKSHEET 73

VALUE	RANK	OBLIGATION	CONSEQUENCE
4.			
5.			

HOW DID I DO TODAY?

To be ethical speakers, we must continually be self-aware. The above exercise is a good place to start. Identifying our values or what we think they are is a crucial first step in self-awareness. We must ask ourselves questions each day like these posed by Thomas Shanks, SJ, PhD[25].

1. Did I practice my values?
2. Did I do more good than harm?
3. Did I treat others with dignity and respect?
4. Was I fair and just?
5. Was my community better because I was in it? Was I better because I was in my community?

---

25. Shanks, Thomas, PhD. *Everyday Ethics*. Markala Center for Applied Ethics. Published in *Issues in Ethics*. http://www.scu.edu

APPENDIX B
THREE LEVELS OF THINKING INTELLECTUAL PROPERTY MODEL[26]

Dave Bricker proposes a "Three Levels of Thinking" model that helps us consider what is original and what is not. It guides us in the creative processes as we choose words and images to represent our ideas.

FIRST LEVEL THINKING

First level thinking describes the "obvious solution." If you are a problem solver, you might choose to represent yourself with a jigsaw puzzle piece or a Rubik's Cube. The problem with this choice is that everyone — including creative professionals — will think of these ideas immediately. From an intellectual property standpoint, research might reveal that these "first level" concepts are already trademarked; their owners might not want you co-opting their inventions or diluting their brands

---

26. Bricker, Dave, http://www.davebricker.com

with your own. Creatively, using "first level" concepts will likely convey that you are anything but unique; you'll join the thousands of other first level thinkers who saw imaginary brilliance in the first thought to cross *everybody's* mind.

SECOND LEVEL THINKING

Second level thinking asks the reader to "connect the dots." If everyone has four-fingered hands, the problem-solver arrives with a basket of thumbs. If the tortoise is racing the hare, the problem-solver arrives with a jetpack. Second level thinking addresses the person who has the problem as much as it does the problem solver, and suggests the benefit of a *relationship* between the two. From an intellectual property standpoint, second level concepts are much more likely to be original. If not, the metaphors and meanings that drive them can often be reworked into unique, trademarkable concepts. Creatively, second level concepts transcend the cliché world of swooshes and globes and puzzle pieces to demonstrate the intelligence, style, and taste of their originators.

THIRD LEVEL THINKING

Third level thinking produces esoteric concepts that demand a lot (often too much) from the viewer or listener. If the dots being connected have likely never been connected before, you're engaged in third-level thinking. I was complaining to a friend about how my wife and daughter are agonizingly slow to get up and on their way in the morning. I compared them to "two jellyfish racing across a sheet of dry ice." Some people visualize the two jellyfish freezing into solid, icy lumps. Most try not to look vacuous. It's a funny joke if you like *that* kind of humor, but it's not the kind of thinking that builds community around a brand. However, from an intellectual property standpoint, it's a fairly safe bet that nobody beat me to that metaphor.

Professional speakers understand the relationship between creativity and originality, and they strike a balance between the two. Even an old idea can be delivered with an original, second-level twist that engages and entertains. Instead of stealing old Dilbert cartoons for your presentation, work with an illustrator to create your own, original version that's different enough from the source material so that you can proudly call it your own.

APPENDIX C
ETHICAL SPEAKER DECISION-MAKING WORKSHEET[27]

Tentatively state the problem or policy to be developed.

1. What are the relevant facts of the case?
   a. What empirical questions are involved?
   b. What facts might not be relevant?

2. To whom are we obligated?
   a. The general public, institutions, professions?
   b. Who is our client?

3. What sources of guidance are available?
   a. Professional codes of ethics
   b. Laws and regulations

---

27. Adapted and included with Dr. Mitch Handelsman's permission, the Ethical Professor and a fine trumpet player. Handelsman, M. M. (1998). *Ethics and Ethical Reasoning*. In S. Cullari (Ed.), *Foundations of Clinical Psychology (pp. 80-111)*. Boston: Allyn & Bacon.

4. Which ethical principles are relevant?

___Representation
___Professionalism
___Research
___Intellectual Property
___Respect & Collegiality
___Confidentiality
___Business Practices
___Diversity

   b. How?
   c. What are the rights of the parties involved?

5. Restate the problem in terms of its ethical issues.

6. What are the alternative courses of action or alternative policies?

7. What are the consequences of each of these?
a. Long and short-term consequences.
b. Benefits and risks
b. What are the probabilities of these consequences?

8. Is each of these possible actions morally consistent?
   a. Would we choose this option if positions were reversed?
   b. What would the decision be if there were no laws?
   c. What if all actions lead to equally good outcomes?

9. What facts would have to change for our decision to change?

10. How might our values be influencing our deliberations?
   a. Can the consequences be valued differently?
   b. Which facts of the case may be disguised values?
   c. What are my personal motivations?
   d. How might I benefit personally or professionally from the alternative courses of action?
   e. Which courses of action will actualize my highest ethical values?

82 THE ETHICAL SPEAKER

APPENDIX D
PERSONAL COMMITMENT PLAN

Great speakers are intentionally ethical. Research and common sense suggest that writing something down makes it more likely that we will think and act on it.

I am willing to commit to doing the following to support an ethical culture for my speaker colleagues, clients, and business community:

APPENDIX E
NATIONAL COMMUNICATION ASSOCIATION (NCA) CREDO FOR ETHICAL COMMUNICATIONS[28]

(Presented here exactly as approved by the NCA Legislative Council, November 1999)

Questions of right and wrong arise whenever people communicate. Ethical communication is fundamental to responsible thinking, decision making, and the development of relationships and communities within and across contexts, cultures, channels, and media. Moreover, ethical communication enhances human worth and dignity by fostering truthfulness, fairness, responsibility, personal integrity, and respect for self and others. We believe that unethical communication threatens the quality of all communication and consequently the well-being of individuals and the society in which we live. Therefore

28. National Communication Association Credo for Ethical Communication. http://www.saylor.org/site/textbooks/Stand Up, Speak Out The Practice and Ethics of Public Speaking.pdf.

we, the members of the National Communication Association, endorse and are committed to practicing the following principles of ethical communication:

We advocate truthfulness, accuracy, honesty, and reason as essential to the integrity of communication.

We endorse freedom of expression, diversity of perspective, and tolerance of dissent to achieve the informed and responsible decision making fundamental to a civil society.

We strive to understand and respect other communicators before evaluating and responding to their messages.

We promote access to communication resources and opportunities as necessary to fulfill human potential and contribute to the well-being of families, communities, and society.

We promote communication climates of caring and mutual understanding that respect the unique needs and characteristics of individual communicators.

We condemn communication that degrades individuals and humanity through distortion, intimidation, coercion, and violence, and through the expression of intolerance and hatred.

We are committed to the courageous expression of personal convictions in pursuit of fairness and justice.

We advocate sharing information, opinions, and feelings when facing significant choices while also respecting privacy and confidentiality.

We accept responsibility for the short- and long-term consequences for our own communication and expect the same of others.

: 88 THE ETHICAL SPEAKER

APPENDIX F
MARGARITA GURRI, PHD, CSP
Keynote Speaker and Consulting Psychologist
Founder, Red Shoe Institute

Rise above conflict
Stand ethically
Harness the power of authenticity

Dr. Margarita Gurri, affectionately known as the Red Shoe Doctor, cultivates practical solutions for impractical problems in good times and bad.

With humor and wit, Dr. Gurri helps organizations, leaders, and teams communicate better to maximize happiness and performance. Innovate short-term solutions and long-term strategies. Reduce stress, increase productivity, and bolster your bottom line.

Founder of the Red Shoe Institute, Dr. Gurri is sought after by corporate, military, and healthcare leaders. A seasoned consulting psychologist, best-selling author, and speaker, she plays with therapeutic humor in interactive keynotes, coaching, and training to heal and energize. Margarita Gurri brings the experience you need to save the day or step up to the next level with a Red Shoe Attitude.

THE RED SHOE STORY

It all started when the Gurri family escaped from Cuba. Limited to only the clothes they wore, mother Beba wore impractical red shoes as a quiet defiance to Castro. Shortly after arriving in the USA, a woman walked up to Beba and declared, "Those shoes make you look loose." Beba stiffened in anger, but quickly relaxed and proudly said, "Jes! I can dance!"

Those red shoes magically harnessed the power of yuckiness with courage, humor, and grace. At the Red Shoe Institute, we help people turn the negativity of life into positive thoughts, feelings, and actions.

This is the Red Shoe Attitude

CONTACT

Margarita Gurri, PhD, CSP
Margarita@RedShoeInstitute.com
www. RedShoeInstitute.com
954-609-9904

92 THE ETHICAL SPEAKER

APPENDIX G
DAVID BRICKER, MFA

Award-winning writer, author, editor, and consultant, Dave Bricker, MFA offers guidance with eloquent writing and smart publishing strategies. His practice revolves around, "helping remarkable people tell remarkable stories."

As a marketer and Adobe Site-of-the-Day Award-winning graphic designer, he creates powerful visual communications, engaging on-screen user experiences, and effective promotions. The lost art of traditional book design is among his creative specialties. His <PubML>® technology brings rich media eBooks to the open web, and empowers anyone to create beautiful eBooks with WordPress.

A university teacher for 15 years, Bricker's programs and workshops include such topics as *Write Right Now: Crafting Powerful Prose, Publish Your Book, All About EBooks*, and *Finding Your Story*.

While sailing thousands of solo miles and crossing the Atlantic in small boats, Dave Bricker developed his appreciation for stories and storytelling. He helps clients and audiences find and tell their stories to add power and magic to their lives and businesses.

CONTACT

Dave Bricker, MFA
dave@davebricker.com
305.908.1350
www.davebricker.com

CPSIA information can be obtained
at www.ICGtesting.com
Printed in the USA
FSOW01n0326190716
22814FS